How I Feel

T0012076

I Feel Excited

By Connor Stratton

level 2
little blue readers

www.littlebluehousebooks.com

Copyright © 2021 by Little Blue House, Mendota Heights, MN 55120. All rights reserved. No part of this book may be reproduced or utilized in any form or by any means without written permission from the publisher.

Little Blue House is distributed by North Star Editions:
sales@northstareditions.com | 888-417-0195

Produced for Little Blue House by Red Line Editorial.

Photographs ©: Shutterstock Images, cover, 4, 15, 18, 21 (top), 21 (bottom), 22–23, 24 (top left), 24 (top right); iStockphoto, 7, 8–9, 11, 12, 16–17, 24 (bottom left), 24 (bottom right)

Library of Congress Control Number: 2020913844

ISBN
978-1-64619-296-0 (hardcover)
978-1-64619-314-1 (paperback)
978-1-64619-350-9 (ebook pdf)
978-1-64619-332-5 (hosted ebook)

Printed in the United States of America
Mankato, MN
012021

About the Author

Connor Stratton enjoys writing books for children and watching movies, such as *Inside Out*. He's always trying to understand his feelings better. He lives in Minnesota.

Table of Contents

playground

At the Playground

We are going to

the playground.

I feel excited.

I wait my turn to go down the slide.

I feel excited.

I know I will have fun.

slide

I am excited to play on the swings.

I have fun when I swing.

I go to the sandbox, and I feel excited.
I play in the sand, and I have fun.

sand

At a Party

We are going to a party.

I feel excited.

There are treats at

the party.

The treats look good.

I am excited to eat them.

There are games at

the party.

The games look fun.

I am excited to play them.

game

17

grandparents

With My Family

We are going to see
my grandparents.

I love my grandparents.

I feel excited.

My grandfather likes
to cook.

My grandmother likes to
play games.

I am excited to cook and
play games.

I read with
my grandparents.
I am excited to see
them again.